T0273085

THE BARE ABUNDANCE

G.F. DUTTON

THE
BARE
ABUNDANCE

SELECTED POEMS 1975-2001

BLOODAXE BOOKS

ISBN: 978 1 85224 589 4

First published 2002 by
Bloodaxe Books Ltd,
Eastburn,
South Park,
Hexham,
Northumberland NE48 1RP.

www.bloodaxebooks.com
For further information about Bloodaxe titles
please visit our website and join our mailing list
or write to the above address for a catalogue.

Supported using public funding by
**ARTS COUNCIL
ENGLAND**

This is a digital reprint of the 2002 Bloodaxe edition.

The poem is the cry of its occasion,
Part of the res itself and not about it

WALLACE STEVENS

ACKNOWLEDGEMENTS

This selection includes poems from the following collections: *Camp One* (Macdonald, 1978), *Squaring the Waves* (Bloodaxe Books, 1986) and *The Concrete Garden* (Bloodaxe Books, 1991).

Acknowledgements are due to the editors or publishers of the following publications in which some of the other poems first appeared: *Action in Airtime, Chapman, The Dark Horse, Harvesting the Edge* (Menard Press, 1994), *Klaonica* (Bloodaxe Books / *The Independent*, 1993), *Lines Review, Malahat Review* and *Verse*.

Many of these poems have been revised since first publication; those extensively revised are marked with an asterisk in the table of contents, with previously published titles noted in brackets. Employment of upper- or lower-case initials in the poems relates to 'the cry of the occasion' and not to fashion or whim.

The author is especially grateful to Robin Fulton, David Purves, Mario Relich and Anne Stevenson for comments on parts of the present selection; any insufficiencies reflect his own.

CONTENTS

II. SEA: *The Pull of the Tide*

III. FOREST: *The Thrust of the Seed*

IV. ROCK: *Facing up to the Stars*

INTRODUCTORY NOTE

This selection is of new verse, uncollected verse and – with a few revisions – representative verse from previous books. I have not ordered it chronologically, but arranged poems of various dates into four groups; each broadly relevant to a named theme. Members of each group fell readily into acceptable sequence. Such a presentation tends to "place" individual poems, and allows a related run of them, or the group itself, to be read as a whole.

The poems reflect a lifetime's campaigning around the reality of metaphor. They are deliberately spare – excess baggage hinders any journey – and despite variety of subject and structure, convey in retrospect a kind of unity; which might, of course, just be the impression they give me, or I gave them. In any event, they certainly record what came up on the screen I was born with.

For, when released from the womb, nest or cage I, like every animal, explored the outer environment: pressing on if rewarded, sniffing wider if not. Being human as well, I explored also my inner one, where arriving data react among themselves and with my processing of them; and where each fresh impression influences, and is influenced by, those already there. You could call such impressions 'science' or 'art', depending on whether imposed or evoked. I find both categories compatible: they build a continuous spectrum of experience.

Because of this accord, and because I consider metaphor as real to the mind as the stimuli invoking it, I shared life with the variety of environments described in the biographical note. These explorations began as parallel enquiries rather than defined Quests, but when 'epiphanies' – in the Joycean sense of sudden revelation – resulted, they surfaced as verse.

The groups in this book cover four themes put together from such verse. Dealing with personal experiences, they reflect a living approach rather than sealed compartments and usefully include some overlap and contrast. The poems of course were not written to fit the groups, which are simply an arrangement for the present book. The arrangement is as follows.

The first group, 'City: The Grasp of the Hand', celebrates fellowship and enmity, the satisfaction and greed of building up or breaking down, and the success or despair of urbanisation – that public and private "getting behind windows", the struggle in a flux of artefact from prehistory to, one hopes, a tomorrow.

The second group 'Sea: The Pull of the Tide' covers the physical flux: that electronic resonance out through the salt blood to the galaxies. We cannot dictate its tides, but swim them, sail them or fish them, helped by a battery of scientific outboards. Though each group possesses its own shores and wishful drownings, its calls of the horizon and its often desperate discipline, this one perhaps presents them most clearly.

The next group 'Forest: The Push of the Seed' meets the biological flux, our own kin among metropolitan blocks, rocks and asteroids. We agree with it, quarrel, exploit it: yet only so far. Too much technique – factual knowledge, and too little insight – poetic intelligence, bring a now familiar retribution.

In the more inclusive final group, 'Rock: Facing up to the Stars', beliefs, faiths, compassions, ambitions, stretch on a cliff of commitment, to climb higher, descend or fall. This cosmically-directed "spiritual flux", uniquely ours, delivers a cold but bracing wind. It declares our significance to the universe.

Each grouping tends, through its particular revelation, to bare the essential unity of what we encounter – not passive union but dynamic equilibrium between originally opposed forces: human and artefact, sea and land, flower and concrete, faith and knowledge. Innumerable examples occur. Such a counterflow may release, in some of us, an 'epiphany' of reconciliation. Poetry, I believe, strives to capture and transmit that.

G.F.D.

The Bare Abundance

To penetrate
the galaxies
vast, minute
within without
the searching mind
is to progress
so far beyond
their circle of dance
spin of excess
you seem to advance
into a night
of nothingness.

Until by chance
some simple bright
coherence grows,
a reassurance
opening out
like sun among
golden young
springtime willows –
like that it dawns,
deep from the root
through shudder of stems
to leaf in the light.

Like that you sight
maybe just once,
calm and complete
against its infinite

the Bare Abundance
the One delight.

The Miraculous Issue

Up from the dark strata
pulsing out through moss
centuries of downpour,
an ever-unfurling spring
alive against the heather,
a bull-nosed sinuous thing
of sunlit question and answer
greening its way downhill
to feed the house clear water.

The faithful on their knees
think it miraculous,
beyond common reason,
in winter warm in summer cool,
quick to bless the season;
when I kneel
wrist-deep in its thrust and passion
my fingers feel
that truth of imagination.

Yet a thermometer
there through the year
reads four degrees always;
regardless where truth lies.
I set my measure,
my sweat, my shiver,
beside that halt of quicksilver,
its fix of realities,
its scale before my eyes.

For the water about my hand
answers to life;
and the living imagination
pulses that mercury column
degrees of belief I mark up as truth
to stand by my mind; when little seems true
but to kneel on steep ground
and grasp at a flow
ceaseless and vanishing as faith.

I

CITY

The Grasp of the Hand

minimal

it is only the simple sunlight
on a fence post
out of the snow.

and I come to set it upright
at the cost
of a single blow.

then I leave them to the sunlight.
one straight post,
trodden snow.

neolithic

I hold my reason
tight in my hand
    for my season
    against the animals.

they crowd round
crossing themselves
    eyes on that stone
    to see what a man does.

they see me fashion
axes arrowheads
    bold succession
    of irreparable windows.

they stand back
watch us take
    that glittering walk
    towards the volcanoes.

street

this is a street,
paved and flat, saying
it leads somewhere.

I shall take it
but not seriously.
it will lose itself

in courts, piazzas
a haggle
of other streets, will end

in some smoking crater.
I shall take it
as if at my pleasure

as if I could choose
Kirkton Cross
or Ballymet

or Gorton Feus,
with this map in my head
this blood in my shoes.

patience

leaf after leaf must fall
into the leaf-choked pool
before that tree stand tall
clean for sunlight of April.

stone after stone come down
before that returning sun
discover no shadow of town,
bare foot not stub against ruin.

and what of the people? they
like us will grow cunning and sly
invent the winter away
light fires in the ice and snow.

Barbarians

To carry long spears
through a country of grass,

wind washing over
gold and silver,

is no new thing
has often been done,

will not shock the bog-cotton.
This is an empire

of grasses and air, far
from the engines of Caesar, it will endure

itch of the hand
another time round. And as for us,

though not of a mind
for deep ores, precise furnaces,

no loss; we understand
the white joy of platinum.

And follow the wind
with iron of our own.

hut circles

once you know what to look for
you see them everywhere,
rings of grey stone among heather
in clusters riding miles
bareback these upcountry hills.

we know so little about them;
single or double walled,
some dozen steps in diameter
next to a fossilised field
with a scatter of cairns to complete them.

and the people – are what you make them,
their entrances carefully placed
regardless of slope or shelter
always to face southeast;
obsessive as us, as confused.

but every black morning in winter
their God would rise up and wake them.

Angle

Old ruins
among hazel trees.
A likely place
to come upon deer –
caves, hollows,
long collapse
behind spring catkins.

One corner rose
a kind of tower,
masonry sheer
ninety degrees
into the sun.
We shielded eyes,
laid down the gun.

Such chiselled power.
We almost swore
that not till its last
white stone was gone
would any beast
or darkness dare
claim refuge there.

And still recall
the dizzying thrill
of Ascendancy.
That was the day
we came upon
the print of our own
lost garrison.

foundation

one does not need
too many toys;
stones and water,
sun, throw in
stars and trees
fruit and lovers and blood –
enough there
to unsettle.

people will gather afraid,
heap walls, beat metal,
not count the cost.
will come at the last
with trumpets and priest
about a spade.

but you outside,
spare
your pity.
above this child we'll build

so fair
a city.

switch

not clever
to look for dawn
under the arc lamps.
along lit streets
night estates
on pavements emptied to brilliance.
not clever under that light
to fix and pity
so streetwhite a child so late
so hurrying his echoes
stumble into
almost sobs, but not
yet sobs. for in this
ambuscade of glare and shutters
grief's as blinded as delight
so fierce tonight
outstares the dawn and suchlike matters.

augury

upon how birds fly
depends a city.
that is why
we are silent

why so many
kneel and pray
others watch
the dawn sky

why government
black important
on the roof
of government house

will not reply
nor face us.
why police
order us home.

decision in high places,
which way the birds fly,
determines Rome.

Safe Haven

An air raid shelter
square in the street.
Packed tight, and last night
somebody chucked a grenade inside it. But

a solidly logical
construction, walls and roof
kept faith,
never a crack.

Standing proof.
Talisman.
And once hosed out
can be used again and again.

Don't mock. Or invoke
Tragic Joy.
Plan the next one
from a human level. Say,

the passing evil
of some casual boy.

Jihad

The road grips tighter
dives beneath
deep water, down to truth

to one faith, one bright path
beckoning miles
of tunnelling wheels, there are men

in every truck every car
they stare straight on
they will get there

they will be first it is a race
to break into Paradise,
it must burst

rise at the end
into some grand
acclamation of sun.

So many of them,
so sworn to arrive, so able to drive
packed with explosive.

parcel bomb

each day
somewhere it happens. at a clap
leaves fly up, boughs break out
scatter the sky
freeze into silence.
see that gap,
explosion over,
turning its puzzle of smoke about
before the screaming and sirens.

each New Year
a son is told by his father
to handle with care
the gift of a calendar.

grown up

three hundred ton of stone
each time, and its exploding
dust. and so has gone
Kirk Wynd, and Caddengait,

unravelled to a lurch
and ashes, blown
high over shouting children
every afternoon.

Tam Gow's in that.
he drives a truck
and grins at them; looks great
in a yellow helmet.

Portrait

Turned in its frame, facing the wall
in a boarded room behind
what is left of a bed, it will
now the visitors have gone

unmovingly attend
what you call absence fixed on its pin
and will not desire tears
or the demolishers' acknowledgement.

People are walking away, cars
re-starting their engines.
The old house burns, an untouched pheasant
flies screaming into the undergrowth.

Cairn

Piled quite fresh
beside the track.

But not a cairn.
A ruin.

Bulldozed into this crush
of bare white stones.

Look carefully.
Some you'll see

less anonymous,
stained black.

They were the ones
of highest importance

a short while back.
They built the chimney stack.

restoration

the fort empty that was
city of the mind and is
stone and broken glass
crowning a green hill, all
measure a tumbled wall.

to pace about that soil,
number that puzzle of stone
is to begin again
an angle against the storm.

whether the plan had been
Babylon or always
broken glass and stone.

whether we both begin
again, or I alone.

museum

not he that made
this necklace, spun the metal, set the stone,
swung and polished it and laid
it clap upon a rock beneath that sun
in that sea air.
he is completed, gone.
but she who took the challenge up to bare
her throat and wear it,
she is here, white neck
and yellow hair, she is the lack
within the silverwork.
is still too near.
her death not done.

Barra

gold hilts are gone, the silk has faded, masts
dredged up are pine
and poor at that. this girl and her few songs
alone refine
bitches and bullies from their flat
disposable hell.
as Speer observed, one must build carefully
to ruin well.

bond

stones were selected
calculated

tapped, trimmed and collated
into this wall.

patted
with hand and trowel

to satisfy
the keenest eye.

that they'll fall
in or out

tanks or horsemen
ride them flat

tomorrow's ocean
cover the lot

is no reason
for regret.

not an occasion
to wonder at.

never a mason
died for that.

east window

every tree
renounced to stone, a
chastity

of arches vaulting
each to each
that long stretch

of chiselled forest.
at night the floor
flowers with candles.

the air is still;
nothing to stir
granite branches.

only the sun
lighting its wheel
recollects confusion;

it makes a great sky
that choirs the wall,
and rising together

glass people
torture to colour
stone's lucidity.

the high flats at Craigston

the high flats at Craigston stand
rawboned in a raw land,
washed by thunderstorm and sun
and cloud shadows rolling on

from the bare hills behind, each one
out-staring the wind;
that every night
cling together and tremble with light.

The Concrete Garden

It takes time
to become set. Before that

you spread it out
smack it, thrust

bright-eyed advances
about the agglomerate, sow

whatever is new,
is bound to grow,

push through
rise to you there – you

regarding from heaven
before the streets stiffen.

Even then, they swear, one mushroom
can break up a pavement.

Call

A furious wind
on the outer estates,
hail and sleet
at the high flats,

the street lights
flickering.
A good night
for visiting,

rummaging, trying
another's mind,
with something else
beating around

to think about,
to get in the talk.
Up at that door
two blocks back

held half-opened,
Jim and his wife,
his smile uneasy
hers the cool knife

sweet to remember.
Aye man come in,
Liz was just saying
you'd look along,

Christ what a bloody
hell of a wind.
He goes before me.
She behind.

tower block

tanked
to a ten storey view,
the glass
bulges. he
backs from that window,
let him sway
lean and watch
circular fish
moon and explore, spit
stony bubbles. what
an aquarium's for
is reassurance. behind him a blue
plummet of sky
breaks white rocks
together in silence.
let him lean, let him stare
let him try
to compare.
his feet itch
on a desperate floor

ten storeys too high
for his reason to reach
where its thermostat is,
or to look for the switch.

Exact Fare Please

A great scutter,
coming on rain
just as it's dark.

Pavements chromatic,
all that brilliance
expounding the gutter.

Luminously
one by one
buses nose in,
destinations
dramatic
above the welter,

offering sure
transitory
golden shelter
numerate,
accurate,
pay-as-you-enter, and

nose out again
crammed to the last
splashed red light;
maybe a spit,
a final despatch,
as the doors closing. But

if you found none
of the right kind of coin
you have to walk home.

When all are gone the dark and the rain
move in with their own
more practised conclusion.

occasion

down what are called streets
the whole corsage of pity
floats by, laughing, after the storm.
the delicate confetti
vanishes into a drain.

doors bang, gears complain,
and after the tyres' disturbance
journeys begin again.
tall houses, with sealed lips,
billow a little, and are gone.

I turn to you sitting beside me
breathless and close. but
you have leant back in your white veil
and your eyes are shut.

new house in the country

I hear black waterfalls
cauldron the horned mountains;
small ferns hide in their roaring,
rocks tremble about them.

in autumn they move downstream
closer. rivers slip past us
silently, ash trees are green;
but it's best that we leave the garden.

the mortar has scarcely set,
timber still tangs of its planing,
boards bang tight underfoot
and a door swings open, framing

plaster gold in the sunlight.
this will be our bedroom.
its window watches the gate.
it will be hung with white curtains.

stone

stone.
like this one,
dug out years ago
when we were building the house.

we couldn't lift it
lever it, blast it so
it lies as we left it,
just where we pass,

grey and silent,
gathering cracks;
eyes, eggs
seething beneath it,

moss and ivy
eager beside it, already
lichen has tried it, it is marked
for life.

I remember it yellow, unblemished,
a growing refusal in the sunlight.
and us kneeling before it
sweating, dismantling its earth.

eden

not a random
heap of stone –
not on this green

undulating meadow
levelled
just where it is.

it has been
carefully once
walls and a roof, that gap

marks the entrance
and that rowan tree
protected it from witches.

three posts today
keep the cattle
from its dangerous well.

II

SEA

The Pull of the Tide

seagate

mountain to black waves
the paving's laid, past snow,
brief forests, to these towers
lit, night-silent, breeding
above their dark; and here
where the dark's too deep to mend,
at the broken edge of midnight
where gutters fall and
footsteps hesitate,
where there might have been an end –
suddenly all is forgiven
the moon rides out and look,
in ancient regular fashion
that masonry climbs down

stone departing from stone
to greet salt water.

After the Flood

Now at last
beginning again.

A wide calm
of mud and steam.

We have passed
from one history

into another,
find it

naked, no
secret or shame. Those

sea-nymphs so
unstintingly bare

dance in the sun, shriek on the shore
each one

Neptune's own
born-again daughter. High time

they were picked up
rubbed down

dried thoroughly. Made fit
to re-enter the water.

ticket

there has been
no summer and the road has ended
at a broken cliff. that hut

should have been the ferryman's
but he is out
and no one in

but an old woman talking to hens
and her son
has a good job in the town

will not be back
maybe the second week maybe
December, that was his car

I did not see
on this bare island with one road,
cliffs at both ends.

high tide

come down from the fields, the houses,
clearing of stone, building of stone
to the one shore, they are
just landing. face the onset

face the great
breaking of laughter, the gull
screaming its way, its cry
that all live on an island. stand

closer together, wipe each hand
clean on an apron, meet
your visitors. they smile
take many photographs

shining and chattering, they
are relieved of the sea.
the profusion that brought them
and that will take them away.

clearances

this shore will never
wash free of people.
suns beat
waves buffet
to no purpose.
it has suffered
the gift of settlement.
absence lasts longer
than emptiness.

birds sit
facing the tide,
fly screaming
across the field-stones.
my turn to tread
where others laboured.

a long seaboard
with few harbours.

its one achievement
undeparted.

perquisite

bay rhymes with bay
impassively
along the coast,
ushered past
by wave drop
yawn of wrack
roll and snore
of reefs, no rock
about the shore
but trembles to
that easy power, froth
rides upon deep lurchers, oar
intrudes with care, with care.

who
are we that dare
to probe like this,
float a wish,
with twenty fathoms beneath us? put

the boat about,
fish enough
for two we've got
out of this rough
moondriven sea.
or if company's sought,
enough for three.

ad majorem Dei gloriam

to make a poem on Uist
however bare however dull
out of bare rock dull sky
bare brown peat and seawind, is
however bare the poem
to hear again keels grating, voices,
heels upon gravel, maybe
summon for an instant
on bare rock beneath dull sky
on memorable peat,
the shining hair, sea-laughing eyes
unreachable lips
that circle the world we had
long futures ago.

however bare a poem, however
roughly handled. if you think
that rhyme could gain, could strike delight
among such boulders
add
the unfelt backwards pain, the bite
of rock against a girl's bare shoulders.

Displacement

Great cliffs are ground
ever to sand,
rise from that infinite
once more land.

Their gulls a spray
climbing high
as time beats time
on eternity.

Some might claim
a breath of prayer
lifts our white minute
even higher.

But close the book.
We both go out,
put the clock back
in its caveat.

We walk alone
where we began
down on the shore,
the old frontier.

A wave comes in.
I throw a stone.
Two events
that break continents.

Squaring the Waves

The harbour is armed with stone
to clasp the passing water
so that within
ships may lie in the sun between
blotted journeys to the moon.

It is a place
to sit and fish from, children race
shouting along it, explore
last week's crack and the fresh
white concrete, it is a gesture
a stretch of the street
almost too far
from the wondering shore.

And do not regret
its endless repair.
There is a price
for the peace of a harbour,
where two tides meet.

back water

rivers believe
in the sea. they

are impatient with bridges,
churches, all debris.

they have a passion
for ocean.

it is dangerous to dam them, to
let them brood;

they will dream and dream
of a great flood

while you sail blue boats
balance red boards

in sunlight across them. how
a breeze will arouse them

the length of a dam! you must excuse them.
it is their mood.

salmon

salmon,
cylinders of ocean,
yet remain
upstream. see them
before they vanish, fish great fish
circling the black vault, the
thunder of white waterfall, kneel
then and watch
deep in that pool; for not again
this side the salt will fathoms burn
so lucidly for you;
nor out of darkness

hugely to you the rising silver turn.

launch

the new and cold
october sea
rinses shells,
rocks headlands slowly.

make today
first of the month
throw a date
on the one darkness.

there is no time
like that of the flood
rising and hinting of ice
for the eye to look forward.

there is no end
in the beginning of autumn
to the glitter of low sun
on the morning waters.

it is not too late
to think of some boat
breasting far out
before the waves freeze.

How Calm the Wild Water

I *whatever sea*

call it the blood,
salt in darkness
fathoming bones;
any tide
at any stones.

call it the ache
to cave hearts, beat
apart islands, break
fresh promises on
any repetition of beaches, call

it the mirror,
the calm glass
behind the eyes,
quietener of ships, ceaseless
with its lovers and its voyagers.

whatever sea, it will again
again return, you being born
with that taste on your lips.
and will drown you
as if you were glad of it.

II *at the beach*

ocean's beyond
disputation,
any obsession

with shells or weeds, long
deliberation of rubbish, it needs
green distancing and those

skilful to swim
its deep temptation rubber each limb
funnel their breath and because

they go far to refuse,
face it through glass.
that way to make clear

their double horizon.
keep them aware
that they stepped from the shore.

III *entry*

this is his dawn.
his time of admission.
when he looks down

and gives his body away,
the burden, when he is hauled
into the cold

persuasion, the pull,
the vanishing pebbles, the whole
alongside procession

pressing to tell
this is it all, this
the final dilution.

his journey to truth.
his hour of conclusion.
and did he expect it?

he surely had met it.
it stops his breath
in recognition.

IV *littoral*

waves beat in,
rocks withstand;
this white ocean
this grey land

play creation
in the round
of the sun's leisure.
and I swim here

take my pleasure
not in sea
not in shore
but one clean stroke

after another.
that wave and rock
pick up, throw back
between them for ever.

v *how calm the wild water*

how calm the wild water
when you are riding it
when you are stroking

the high white haunches,
when you are in control;
the little while

you are deciding it,
the rocks' howl
quiet at your heel.

when you have thrust
to the silent centre,
where the heart would burst.

This is a dive;
the urge to within
the reach to believe,
try it, it will begin

dark, clamorous,
belabouring,
weeds will implore you
fishes and faces

beat at your head –
ignore them,
you will heed
only what struggles to meet you

the plain stare
of the sea floor, a square
of your own measure,
it will greet you

hug you with rarities,
sandgrain and stone
clutch of white shells. Then
dismiss you again

back to the surface to pour
shell stone and sand
out through your hand
into indifferent water. Nor

anything more. That was your dive.
That was belief.
Being achieved
for the price of a breath.

it is a sea urchin, bristling
in the sun.
it prickles my peeled

fingers, it worries
in waves of retraction;
I plucked it

deep from some laminarian,
blooming spiky and crimson
out of the shiftiness

unlikely as a chrysanthemum.
and should I carry it home?
that would be uncomfortable

for both of us, I should be forced
to boil it in caustic, scrub it
all afternoon

free of its ruined jelly. when dry,
a pink and purple and white
adoration of symmetry,

I could repopulate its mosque-work,
thread it with memory,
prickles and agitated feet,

set it on a shelf
in the front room by the windowseat
among dead photographs

slowly to lose its
echo of sea.
it would go with those faces.

it flutters down, it pauses
once to remain
a flower in darkness. is gone.

VIII *storm*

however far down
on the sea floor:
you hear the storm.

in the moving silence
of fragments to and fro,
in the slow resistance

of the great stem
you are clinging to.
but nothing more.

and the small fish
look up as they pass
at the desperate visitor.

IX *Delegate*

A mile off the crowded shore.
Not near. Not far.

Enough for a swim.
And to wave to them from,

to goggle their eyes
at the end of a glass.

They do not approve
my living above

such a deep underneath,
they mind

my treading on their drowned.
A mile off the crowded shore

rocking alone, about to postpone
tomorrow's midnight below.

Drawing a line
at what I will do.

I will float in the sun, nothing more,
lie as I am till the tide runs on,

shoulders me in
through darkening foam and the evening skerry.

Only a mile.
And today is no hurry.

All this I will tell them, and they will smile;
and towel my trembling body.

he could be seen
far out in the waves.
a private war. between

himself and himself
and no concern
of theirs. and yet they gave

turning away
some little thought
to what might be the bay

he'd be washed up at,
even land in,
and if landing what

wet doorstep he'd be standing on,
and where his clothes would be
and what his name.

XI *return*

I come from the sea.
there is salt on my lip.
I have lain on the sand
in the waves' retreat,
I have raised myself up
and trembled, been met
by battering light,
untouchable air;
and still stand here
bearing my weight,
trying to re-gather
trying to command
foot after foot
to climb the shore,
persuade my mind
to understand
why I must suffer
myself to land.

Up from the sea's rock –
you know the trick – fields
houses, look

a blue frock,
that child
regards you, holds

upside down its doll,
tries out a smile. You're halfway back,
follow the track

beyond, hard familiar ground,
you're going well, a whole school
plays football, through the noise

your last gull
cries and cries
with no voice. The land

you started out from, and the crowd
is cheering, on parade,
knows nothing about you. Time

to pocket stone,
put on boots of iron,
tramp across and join them.

waves have gone back

the waves have gone back.
children come down from the mountains and play
quietly on the sands or run shouting in the black
dripping caves. today

things are re-found,
people resume, clean up the lighthouse
dry out machinery, even the drowned
do not roll eyeless

about the coast
but assemble, talking dispassionately
in some great gathering ground.
the unborn are not lost.

III

FOREST

The Thrust of the Seed

cutting trail

I cut this trail
through young pine.
they climb up past me
to the sun.

I make the same
journey too,
axeing darkness
here below

peering ahead
where no one has been,
either side
where no one will go.

faith

I

branches fail.
the track's forsaken.
trees fall.
the house is broken.

plant on.
chance knows season.
this is April
without question.

chance is sure.
its random year
sets the dates
each side your lifetime.

tall the oak
rough its bark.
its roots
consume silence.

II

I need no lifetime to enjoy
the flower that drinks its day of sky

or years of frost and hurricane
to praise the seed and plant again

for calendars no more apply
now I grow old and make my way

out of less likely spring after spring
into whatever is certain to be

far from this winter-blossoming
downside of eternity.

Dignity

These young birches
shriek green laughter up the hill
billow on billow. They
stop as he enters. He
carries his promised absence
carefully and yes
he does seem slow
but the end of life
is dignity what though
birches toss their impatience and
the spring sun's at his back like a knife.

This wood's enough
to practise silence in
and let him go.

Hazard

A hazel tree
at the kerb of Seggie Way,
survivor
of what was formerly
Seggie Brae, alive here
by accident, decidedly
now no longer
permitted to stay. For
the road bends, it offends
blocks the view
of such a corner. And after
the earth mover
no sign
that it grew, a smooth green
safer distance, somewhat more
predictability. The cautious eye,
ageless raviner,
has picked the corner clean.
Can see
clearer than before
the end of the day.
The further difficulty in the sunset.

hazels

dry leaves
under the hazels,
bare stems, stirring,
a bare wind
and a bare sky
on a bare day
dropped into winter.

no sound
no birds about,
bareness profound

but for the green delight
of a hazel tree
fresh in my mind

and in the hazel nut
on my bare hand.

After

Not the sight of it
after the storm.
Not the oaks thrown, their
tangle of branches, not
the sun through them
steaming the long roof-tree,
still firm.
But the breath held,
the great light of it,
and a silence the sound
of a horseman's hand
soothing repeatedly
some tremble of haunches.

ash tree

so
it is down.
sawn up and gone.
a huge absence,
as after thunder.
neighbouring branches
stretch and explore,
blackbirds thrushes
kick up the fingerbones,
I for my share
watch that great head swinging
dizzy with memory

and know my bare eyes
the poor october things they are.

Roots

It too has gone, that tall blue pine
that moved so out of line
at every gust
it one day would come down

across the house. I planted it
the year my son was born.
Today I let
him make the first and deepest cut.

When we took up the roots we found
they were long, perfectly sound
and the better to grip had curled
and split a great stone undergound.

Sufficient

Together we felled that tree,
cut it, split those logs,
stacked them to dry.

It took seven men to grow
and now for seven weeks
will warm us two.

Seeds break out to the stars,
a thousand already as we
pull up our chairs.

Poking at flame and spark,
scarlet with seven men's sunlight,
backs to the dark.

Trees

He often wrote about
felling trees
and planting them.

As when he cut down
a fifty foot larch
he put there at nine inches

and planted a pine
at four and a half. That
is not to create.

It is what he was writing about.
A weeping of forests
from one genesis.

After Brashing Pines

Brashing is
lopping off dead branches, old
entanglements, outgrown

gestures, so your trees
rise calm and clean into their own
September. When

you leave them, go home
they resume
high business, needle on needle

repeating, gathering
the night wind, and
you do not mind

you do not look behind
at what's beginning again, what storm,
what growing collision of darkness.

You have no concern,
the job being done
and they putting up another season,

the tall leaders
quarrelling together
against their stars.

Plantation

The besieging innocent
graze nearer.
Implacable deer
intractable rabbit.
They will devour.

Lord of fresh leaves
your estate does you credit.
They started the war.
You must exhibit
imperial habit.

Do not despair.
Tighten the wire.
Stand by your gun.
Especially in spring
cherish iron.

That is what
empire's about.
Six hectares of crop
coming up
for redistribution.

Weed Species

These are the trees
that grow straight, seed
of knowledge, planted, fed,
tended line by line to be

felled in a gale
of sawdust and petrol. Not those
over the fence, sown free,
broken by season, strays

swarming with eyes and evasion
pests and diseases, the wry
birch and aspen. Beautiful
weed species.

Timber Line

In that Welsh verse
sung a thousand kings ago, its name
I can't remember, flame
was blazing half a tree and burst

spring green the other half
perpetually. Magic once,
now that image blunts
sudden against my thought as on the path

this rock my boot. We've stopped. Here's timber line.
That fir's a hundred years
and four foot high. One side's bare
the other, halfway brown.

Dialogue

Enough spruce
cut this winter,
enough ice
and crushed needles, air
biting with resin.
Enough that's brilliant,
sawtooth. What else
on offer?
          I pause
join deft flit
of a robin
about piled branches,
wary of stem-juice;
on the lookout
for rare softness,
something of use.

Both of us
warmed by winter;
and near but no nearer
than searching the snowglare
for something other
than sawdust and spruce.

Birds

Birds present the problem
in its most immediate form.
Pipe-legs, feathers,
whisper of breath
cocked eye and beak.
Underneath –
a puffed throat,
imminence of note
unbearable. Dismiss them.
They can whistle
elsewhere. Birds
are a quick urge
of greed and seasons.
For those reasons
deserve respect.
Tamed, are abject
flutterers to be despised.
I cannot understand

why I am pleased
when they feed from my hand.

violets

violets are cruel, with pale
demanding scent.
wet grass displays its knives, birds
shriek argument.

all is fresh and bitter as
an apple's core.
I put the new day by, go back
to you still there

standing at the gateside glad
the morning is so fine and glad
to see me on so fine a morning glad.

emperor's walk

no
I am not heroic, I prefer
not to conquer
polar regions, my
gardens in July
serve for me.

I do not have to be
choked with snow
to understand zero.

and of course it is
gratifying to see
those great cedars I planted,
evergreen
acres of them, such a fine
memorial, but in some ways

I should like to die
clean.

annuals make
the best subjects.

pioneer

he named the unknown mountain. now
its frost
takes care of the east. out
in a deckchair wrapped in a rug
he savours new zeros. his grandchildren
tiptoe past. spring has begun.
the daffodils they brought him
crisp in a jug
untwist, take flower

melt green in the sun.

A Pointed Spade

You need a pointed spade
for ground like this.

To be of use
in this last rock and turf.

A square-edged blade
so good to double-trench

that first allotment
would be bent

never penetrate
this kind of earth.

You need to wrench
then drive it straight

lever to and fro
spoon up the stones

deep as you can go.
An inch or two to start

then once you're in,
no doubt.

But time, and finding soil to fill
the hole you've lifted out.

Culture

Just to choose
a corner of the wilderness
is to enclose
it with intent.

Is to create
garden, gardener
a life spent
cropping the rubble, a desire
to regulate
what goes by,
catch at a scent, ensure
some branch against the sky.

Is to incur
from the first day
what creation cost, the haste
to cut and tear,
rake things over.
At the least the need
to look about, decide
what wild flower
that once had led you there

is now a weed.

drought

soil is dry.
roots meet rock;
stem, bare sky.
day after day
God's blue eye
measures the earth again.

pray it were gone
and clouds come on
easy with rain.
that prayers could be done
and seed put down.
eternity wither to green.

a garden has not courage
to be desert.

pleasaunce

they keep their distance
although I planted them
although I protect them
from slug, vole, the particular malice
of climbing mice,
the slash of pheasant.
not to mention deer
that once through the wire
would strip the place bare.

flowers flowers
from Oregon, from the Himalayas,
bored with my bad soil
reward my toil
sparsely, are lost
in deprecating leaves.
my summer is what it achieves.
were it not for the frost,
rocks, teeth, rasping tongue,
the living virulence I live among
I would throw down
spade and pen,
cry off this slapped rump of a mountain.
go back to earnest discussion.
take a room in town.

Docken

And there is a docken
that each year
grows hugely in a corner
of the carpark, that has seen

three factories take on this site
and has outlived
all three, survived to be
just now Japanese, it is

a great favourite,
old Willie Stout
the gardener does not dare
spray it or howk it out.

A docken, a survivor.
With a long stem
that reaches from
the secret to the sun.

Campanula latifolia 'Alba'

Is a tall
steeple of white bells climbing,
sounding out

carillons purple
at the throat, rooted
in a rosette

of devoted leaves and chiming
peal after peal crystal
all June evenings until

petals are shed
and globes of green seed
hang silent below.

Then the name must make do.
It is tied to the stem every season,
and tries to ring true.

Serpentine

A kind of path
that won't pursue the truth
about a garden,

cannot square
with such severe
enclosure, but would rather

seek to please, gather
flowers, trees,
repeat the views

of every daily
dilly-dallier. It lies
so easy, is so busy

setting out
sequence of avoidance
through the green plot that

a shock to find
suddenly its end
bare wire. And

maybe an iron gate.
To go further,
you open that.

Roses

That's what roses are for.
A rose is there
to keep you to the corner

so you go
where God's concrete
tells you to. No

sneaky-foot
short cut here,
a rose bush is razor-bare

it'll scare
you dead sober
you'll think twice

before you leave
the set truth
the public path. The public rose

blesses those
precast ways
with leaf and flower.

Should you dare
pick and choose
it drops all that

will bite and scratch
full stretch
at your track.

A rose bush is
a coil of wire
that needs care

any night
to beat flat
pull right out.

You think of it
days after.
Each time you come to a corner.

Joy

Twenty-seven bullfinches
in one week
of sun

visited the blossom –
so sparse
now the years

close in – of his cherry trees
from Japan. They enjoyed
each opening bud

as much as he did, not
for the whiteness
not for food

but for the delight
of ripping them out
and throwing them down, a circle of white

blenching the grass
under each tree. Pure
anarchy, sheer

destruction. There was something about them
misusing the sun
for private joy

that offended his sense
of our common inheritance. And must have been why
each day, he shot them.

Twenty-seven bullfinches
In one week of sun. The best,
almost, with that particular gun.

against the sun

a clatter of stained glass.
that pheasant climbs
red october air
bracken-winged. who aims,
crashing his gun, finds there
blue smoke, gapped silence.

see him go
carefully, not
look upward. he must know

he has broken a window.

Michaelmas

It is good
to return from exuberance,
along with the weather
to dead grass
brown heather
water clear enough
where it is not frozen.

August was too
bellyripe and breathless,
made scenes.
The children cried.
Nothing demeans
like fecundity.
It is good to return to no leaves.

The door swings open,
the woman shakes across the step
overcoats, scarves.
The house is dusted
floor to shelves.
The summer plants are turned out,
their pots thoroughly scrubbed.

Death in October

Good to go off in colours.
Scarlet before the sleet;
fuming crimson, shrieking orange
a relaxed butter-pat

yellow. Name them. Anything
is better than flat
worn-out green. Even that
is strangely remote

in frost lying on the white
grass, whiter
edged, each vein
picked out for the last time, crystalline.

silences

there are no silences
in autumn silences.
where you can hear a leaf fall
on to other leaves
and the wind blows silence in the bare boughs
fiercely, and the river
bundles its brown
flood of silence over the rocks.

there are no silences
but my own silence
beating about me,
heart among the deafnesses
in this season of loss.

and what is that beating in my silence
but the beat of the silence when it stops?

Thicket

Raspberry bramble nettle
great field thistle.
Even dwarf willow.

In summer
quite intractable.
You can't get through.

You must wait for the snow.
Snow smooths everything level.
Is above all argument.

Then you walk straight on
hear stems crackle
leave footprints for the moon.

reassurance

a black wind
has cleared the snow.
the ground
sobs and is soft again. go

higher and find
eight months' frost,
wind
white and faithful to the last.

who shall escape the hound
that paces about the winter
at the back of a man's mind?

Tundra

These two-foot trees at the limit of life
set out to prove
the truth of a root, achieve
branches against the blast, hold fast
winter by winter
deliberately bare
so they wrap sure, carry safe
to the next up-cry of sun
a pure fountaining green;
their seeds extend, countermand
this waste of land, find their end
beyond the tracks
of the last visiting fox.

Others advance the persistence,
engine the flight;
across this blue
high arch of morning white
dedicated lines fan out,
each one true
to its unseen light.
Drawn to bestow
a still further
cargo on distance.

On Passing

No it is not repeat
repeat, it is once
only and enough.

These juniper berries bunched,
sun-bosomed through the frost-
needles in the bright

snow-light, meet their first
chance to last next
spring, and no more;

rounded-off tough
sky-blue-bloomed, their green
one-year-behind

successors crowding about them.
It is enough
to have seen a stiff

laden juniper branch,
pausing as you are
passing, just now once

out of the snow and never,
coming back how often,
to see it this way again.

The prize the primacy of it
the instantaneous thousand
cold needles ever

afire and berries
thrusting their one spring
aware out of the cluster.

Your own passing and theirs
together, stars
in the eternal glitter.

interstadial

once more that sand is extended
the glacier done, ended,
the blue snout the great ox-weight
absolved to silver and sunlight, once more
an absence relaxes,
settles for peace.

before the return of the fuss.
before moss
grass and the marching rootmat.

before the rush
of the first forests, before
the first axes.

IV

ROCK

Facing up to the Stars

fault

city, sea
and forest. all
rooted on rock.

only we
discover the crack,
try to climb up
try to climb down
stretched out alone
at the heart of the break

each logical grip
a grope towards luck.

and you complain
                at the window
my verse is not sufficiently explicit,
does not reflect
                the human situation.

of only a single poem

above the plains
mountains flourish,
white, distracting eyes
from lower compulsions.

they are cold, frequently
dangerous, always
exhausting and when you come down
are still there.

then why climb them?
ask your constituents
ask the headbellies ask
the paunchbrains. not knowing

what it is to represent them
what it is to be the guest
dirty unapologetic

of even a minor pinnacle.

Belief

So that is their mountain.
A trodden disgrace.

The whole face rubble,
the track a struggle

stone to stone, each intention
slides back down. Surely they need

a staircase laid, of regular tread,
leading their feet

straight to the summit. But
they would cry out, never forgive

their elevation
interfered with,

made safe. They put weight
on the doubt.

A heap so rotten, you'd never believe
it could reach this height.

solo

a day to try
the route direct, those crags collect

no thunder, sky
impeccable blue, no gods to crack

that clean white rock, no winds to cry
about its sharpness, no one by

to check how near the top
he who set it up

climbs with delicate hands
gap to gap

glad of the almost absence.

Crossing Over

Stones still grip
both banks, build up
squared assured

complete the arch; pledged
to centuries, old
ash roots, boulders, huge

shadows of pools. An obstinate
narrow bridge
cobbled and steep

it was replaced
by a simple flat
iron one, set between

two cubicular
precast abutments, well clear
of the nervous water; concrete

white, iron green, vanishing
either side
into the road unseen

by any driver. Proud
to make no fuss
crossing over.

Intersection

They have swum here
from deep blues off Greenland,
silvering clear
through salt and waterfall to lie an hour
under this bridge and soon
will beat up the rapids, vanish again
back to the bare
progenitive mountain.
Water slams down
clamouring past them
cold for its ocean, they in their line
playing, evading, tethered to upward. We lean,
we greet them
prisoner to prisoner meet them
one minute together
here in mid-river, a pause
silencing Time
this calm April morning. Then move on
to the opposite shore, the steepening climb
the grey stone house
we meanwhile call our own.

Border

This is the Border,
like many another. An old wound

not yet healed, a fault
of geology maybe

or weather. Land
tossed about, crushed between

mist and rain, sleet and sun,
long brown

winding-on
summits of confusion. Ending in

the same black storm.
Nights heavy

with reconciliation
dawns clean

with the old bright treachery. And I
for life must stand

on this twice-turning roadway
lashed by a two-faced wind and these

fierce roses that have climbed
down from each bank and rise entwined

before, about me
and behind.

Recycling

On his seventieth birthday they gave him
a new History of Scotland, one more
shovelful of debris
off the floor

of this particular cage
of Godstained monkeys, life
chewed to the last
tossed crust

and dropped from above. They were sure
this present of the past
would feed what future
seventy had in store.

He thanked them, being aware
how difficult it is
to meet eyes
across even a single year.

Then all went out
into winter sunlight
and planted another
of his young trees.

Treading down
the good earth, the tough
relief
of the last sod.

Small branches
thrust against evening.
Conversation
followed into the house.

Genesis

To compose
pibroch among eviscerate
volcanoes
as once they did on Skye and Mull was not
seeking to articulate some void
but rather conjure from that cold stone bed
what thread
what one pure tune
might lead them up to light. For yes
as if by plan
eruption follows eruption and those fires
have forged in all of us
a labyrinth to outwalk chaos
and time our pace.
That music is continuous,
conducting chance along our course,
the silent antiphon.
It gave the measure to their guess.
Listen. Each gracenote steps in place.
There are no fragments in our universe.

passage

it faced the north with a roar, then
ran snivelling southward, long
green dribbles into the sun
where cattle were happy, men
had called it Alba,
Caledonia, briefly
talked of it as Scotland, now
it empties under our wingtips,
five minutes of wrinkles,

a dusting of snow.

as so often in Scotland

as so often in Scotland
the sun travelled
dyke over dyke, burning
dead grass golden and ending,
after a wallow of foothills,
on one brown summit;
that flared its moment, too,
and was gone.

Flat

Like much of Scotland
this is a flat land,
stretched between
mountains and shore
grey cloud grey haar
most of the year
and has been
no doubt
often as flat
though shrugged about
various seas
dipped and raised
time again,
kindled, braised
iced to the bone.
Nevertheless
smoothed with pale green
under a weak sun
and offered to
what we'll call human
it had its attractions.
Whether or no
any remain
or any new
have come in
is less certain.
These constructions
dot it sadly, though
big at the foot,
for this is not
climate for concrete,
and mud
too soon succeeds
ideas of grass.

People and weeds
have to thrive here,
roots and seeds
have to explore
momentary silt.

Have to cherish
leaf or even flower
of the one result.

Penalty

Natural
to play football
in a flat land
pointed and planned,
where streets invite
anguish at edges, wounds
from whatever surrounds.
Inevitable
some Saturday night
to come by a ball
that would bounce and roll
far on the flat
and to stop all that,
teach it drill,
trap it, keep it
spot-lit, still,
sized for a goal.
And only fair
to play it square,
even the score.
To kick by rule
strike that ball, net it while
cries rain down and
streamers fall
acknowledging out of the darkness.

They cheer us yet, gather about our
stamping and mismanaged feet.

goal

a child
kicks that ball
field after field

following it, his play
to banish distance;
older, every day

more accurate,
will try
to lodge it in some net

having been taught
at school
the game of the rule.

he will miss
he will miss
so often

until he's forgotten
to miss the day
he scored every foot of the way.

visitation

above the long street
mornings gather.
as likely this house
as another.

as likely to
receive the sun
as houses that
believe in one,

that do not need
to ask if dawn
adds a darkness
of its own

or whether it
be cruel or kind
crossing the windows
of the blind.

still life

flies,
the vile animate,
beat on the glass.
open it.
let them out.
in two hours the twelve hour frost
ends them. dust
thoroughly, a last
polishing, my corners must
be clean.

this afternoon
I frame the sun,
focus the one
host of heaven
on my room. then

tonight at the pane
the inside ice
is for me alone.

crumbs

at Donald Street
she'll pull the brown bag out, throw bread
to pigeons on the road.
The birds have insolent eyes,
the sun its one cold stare
from colder skies
for Donald Street, Caithness, Kintyre –
whatever Scotland's underneath
this Christmastide –
Butt of Lewis, Barra Head
Barvas where her brothers died

black stone of Cowdenbeath

white towers of East Kilbride.

so praise is given
beneath one arc of that declining heaven.

eine feste burg

(Berlin 1970)

underneath
a white wall,
slab of concrete
broken wreath
bent cross recall
whatever grief
had gained that height
before it fell.

or found relief
aiming so well.

frontiers

but for wire
pieces of tar in the grass
you'd never have guessed

a bridge once crossed
somewhere near here.
it is like peace

it is like a beginning,
the electric fence
makes little difference, that river

has ever been
too swift between
for easy swimming.

Fracture

I *fracture*

A very small table.
Not even a meal.

Just two glasses on it
both empty and I

am about to explain
there is wine in them still

when you smile and you lean
closer and closer and then

the table is over
and both glasses broken.

No reason for guilt,
nobody's fault,

they are busy with cloths and apologies.
But you have destroyed my metaphor.

And I cannot take my eyes
from your eyes.

II *Family Break*

It is the first
full day of summer, skirts
of dizzy young trees

lift to a dead
breeze, they drop again
it is the June

holiday, it's why
this silence and the sad
road empty. Only one

packed Ford the last in town
blasts through the echoes, a child's arm
trails from its window, all rush on

to sky-high noon
brassed sun
leaves of leather. How soon has gone

white-shouldered dawn, that rare
just once together seen
imminence of summer.

A barbarous light
bursts in from the street.
Dismisses our half-hung curtains.

III *Weekend*

Lights pick up,
lay aside,
as if for ever
pieces of road.

Wheels
banish them.
They are the same
ache of gravel

we walked upon.
That when we are gone
will come together,
making a dawn.

And us by then
asleep in some town.
Travelled how far,
as if to get nearer.

IV *Forecast*

Out of the grey
indicative east comes wind
this withering morning, we
shall have snow soon.

It dies down.
And he has gone
over the moor
back to beyond.

She turns away
settles her dress,
almost a hush
as she goes in

almost no stir,
here and there
the breath of a guess
to brush off the skin.

Up in that room
against the pane
the same question
stares again

searches the sky
as if to see
heart and heaven
in harmony.

Winds gather
patter the glass;
blot the weather
blind the face.

This is the weather
December makes. Like this,
like this with a few flakes,
winters begin.

v *Open Cast*

It will all be put back
just as it was before.

At present, my dear,
it may be a scar
an open wound, a hole in the ground

a quarter mile square:
that's nothing to fear –
we have mended, all round,

holes that were,
filled them in by the million ton
hammered them down

to hectares of beautiful green, each one
rolled out between – how far, how far –
high-tensile wire;

and simply alive
with mutton and beef.
You'd never believe

how solid they are, how safe
with the ashes tucked underneath.
And this hole here

will be as pretty a place –
you'll recognise
the lane, the flowers, the trees

the field with the blue butterflies. And yes
you will love her as much as your mother, so please
don't cry any more.

It will all be put back
just as it was before.

Lachie

The roof lasted
a little longer than he did.
They sold the sheep, the beasts

went to the knackers, the tractor almost
too rusted
to move. He lived on

in drink and conversation,
guffaws, a hundred
tales of wit

and prowess fading slowly,
as the place itself had foundered
into one more green

nettle-making heap; but that
an architect bought it,
for weekend use,

with a professional wife
three small children
and a dog called Simon. Saturdays

from the hill the house
smokes at evening again,
fresh-painted, with a new straight roof.

They sold his sheep, the beasts
went to the knackers, the tractor almost
too difficult to move.

Time

Autumn
strips the decorations
from a roofless house.   Spring
pins them up again.

Each summer
however
the walls stand lower.

Something
is spoiling the picture.
Not keeping time.

Shelter Stone

A kind of cave.
A shelter stone.
Twenty ton
leaning against the cliff.

Welcome enough
in blizzard or rain
or as a howff
to keep the icy stars off

and shelter your light.
You sleep safe under granite.
Out of the dead weight
of the open night.

clach eanchainn

that great stone
the shape of a brain
twisted and left there

out on the moor,
crystals and fire
fisted within it,

often has seen
forests go down
their soil squandered,

seeds blown in
blown out again,
ashes and iron

beneath it surrendered.
it was begun
with the first star

is now a stone
sheltering foxes
out on the moor.

often have men
marched through the dawn
to give it a name.

Vandal

A long way up, and at the top
a view and a sign –
Ancient Monument – that green
overgrown circular heap,
once a crown ruling this hill
and now worn down to its own moraine,
memorial of Bronze Age will,
of rough stone summoned to rough stone,
hand after hand in a chain.

Voices gone, order forgotten,
stone after stone fallen away,
should I – visitor, inheritor –
as my part in the procession
as this afternoon's assertion
kneel and replace
one two three of them
into some likely space? Yet
any that fit
raise more doubt.

Maybe just pass by, obey
the downhill certainty,
the run of luck; take the track
out of their wreck,
drop free of them.

That would deny
responsibility. I come
at the end of a long climb, today
troubles my feet, let me create,
be surrogate; let me try
if high authority
still caps this site – step back,

grow King enough myself to kick
as royally
as randomly about

all that I see of them.

Ruins

To set three stones
together in the sand
and rake them round
is to reduce
the odds on emptiness

make us a place
to meditate,
to gamble on the great
It-Might. Above the town,
along the beach,

rocks unassigned
randomly crouch,
cry for composition;
beseech us to guess
their anguish for order,

what might be gained
once they were tuned
by a single touch. But ruins –
ruins won't join in the play;
bids were too high

a previous day, their ashes
indicate loss, their wager
is over, they lie in despair
of raising another. They ask us
just to forget

the chance of an absolute.

ceremony

there is always
ceremony. sheathing,
unsheathing, symmetry
about the green wish, autumnal
fires. down this ward
too
succession is orderly, doors
slide backward, lights switch on, cries
go dumb with needles, become
                as you turn from that window
stars in a black sky.

it is just protocol.
an obligation
christening every funeral.

November in Angus

No flab in this landscape. No cushion
for bones. Just muscle.
And the fat
packed tight
into corners for the winter.

For eyes to scour, claws
to seize, white
teeth to bite. A store well hidden,
to its last brown
hazel nut.

The sun a cold red stone
sinks down. Snow too,
bough to bough.
No room on loan
for a visitor.

Leave your crumbs leave your crumbs.
A scatter, a gesture, from Edinburgh, one
shrug from a bag. They lie there,
thumbed, half-eaten, more than enough.
Squirrels will finish them off.

outside

the sky clears,
looks at the snow.
stars
visit broken branches.

ice narrows
the window pane.
tomorrow
there'll be avalanches

from roof and hemlock;
not tonight.
one look's
enough. to bed and let

them face it out
in tight silence.
what
they battle about, forget

just for a little.
night's too brief
to settle
griefs beyond the curtain.

we lie awake
with a sleeping child.
each crack
adjusts the roof's burden.

Bulletin

The glaciers have come down
dead white
at the end of the street. All over town

cold mist of their breath,
and along gutters
water runs

freezing beneath. But
the machines are out, lined up,
beautiful, their great lights

tossing back darkness. And the engineers
have promised to save us,
they have left their seats

for a last meal, when they return
all will be well, under control,
it is their skill, listen –

already upstairs
they are teaching their children
to sing like the ice.

exit

the trees went out
one by one
then the grass, only the lichen

remained, food of the dead
reindeer, that used to
welcome it out of the snow.

to behold the junipers

when snow has lain
week after week,
been soldered down,
its ice will break

slowly, deliberately,
branches. but lower
branches only.
branches higher

swing green till the next
snowfall. meanwhile
birds gobble blue berries in sunlight,
roots do their best
to be careful.

until
out of the mind of winter
the trodden seed
as if it were nothing but some new idea
springs back again.

in memoriam George Forrest
(1873–1932) plant hunter

here are the gorges,
mekong, yangtze, salween,
yellow between
long green
shudders of the himalaya.

up from the boil
the steam,
to the stone bowl of the snowline climb
the rhododendron jungles, toil-
ing back into silence.   here the

great waxed separate
primitive scented
blossoms, white, white
studded with crimson, gold, blood-
red, rising slowly, shed
monsoons from elephant leaves,
fictolacteum,
irroratum, vernicosum, each receives
tapping of sunlight on

long-deliberated petals.   here
his kindly host old Père Dubernard dispensed
communion, was taken
out from the smooth trunks praying,
both arms broken,
robbed of nose and eyes,
picked naked to pieces
three nights and days,
staked in the ashes
of his mission.   here

the so precious
seeds
were gathered up, despatched
according to the needs
of the distant professors,
the business men
with large crying gardens. here
he died
'on his last trip', satisfied,
suddenly, beside
his gun, his dog and a pheasant.
is buried
at tengyueh. here

because
india butts asia,
summits rise
brokenly
metre by metre
into untenable skies,
clutching their ice together,
and the great trees,
the extended stigmata,
ride obediently
up the steep valley. here

the snow plume flies
night and day
over the last white stations,
over the buried disarray,
bursting icefall, twisted alloy,
fossils and fragments, cylinders, ropes,
fluttering shreds
of the expedition tents.

exposure

it is the great
adequacy.
and looks in through the kitchen window
while the bread is being cut.

beneath it
the lewd earth turns restlessly.
it will go away
but must come back because what else

is as white as snow or calls
with delicate immensity
to help us bury the summer?
treat it kindly. do not doubt it.

we would never be done without it.

Finale

I

What?
Not finished yet?
Still at the ballot?
Do I still try
try again
for clear sight
through clouding eye
minute on minute,
as it to delay
as if to deny
that crunch?

Junkies of adrenaline
vote out such doubt,
they see it straight,
it's fight or flight for them,
fist or olive branch
against their sky — but I,
after all I've said,
how can I conclude
one choice right?
Both ways
sign our Fate

set our Cross
against the asteroid.

II

Meanwhile
I choose a stone
that satisfies my hand
and fling it clean
into the centre of the mirrored pool
and watch
sunlight on the intermingling ripples
lapping each
promontory, isolated rock
half-unseen shore
and the sudden still-cascading track
of one disturbed white bird
that now wings far
into the untouched, disappearing, westward.

G.F., G.J., G.J.F. or **Geoffrey Dutton** (1924-2010) was born on the Welsh borders of Anglo-Scots parentage and brought up in the Scottish diaspora. Apart from much global travelling, he lived thereafter with wife and family in Scotland, the passionate austerities of which compel his poetry – helped by many other lifetime environments, including mountain, sea, forest, industrial tenement, hillside shack, various arts and the intercontinental circuses of biomolecular research.

Major publications fed by what he called 'this metaphorical imperative' cover solo longdistance wildwater snorkel swimming (*Swimming Free*, Heinemann & St Martins Press, 1972); mountaineering – his 'classics of wit and humour' *The Ridiculous Mountains* (Diadem) and *Nothing So Simple as Climbing* (Hodder) were combined as third edition in *The Complete Doctor Stories* (Bâton Wicks 1999 reprint); and his 44-year 'ecological dialogue' with a few rocky windblasted East Highland acres led to various articles, radio and TV features and the acclaimed pair *Harvesting the Edge* (prose and verse, Menard Press 1995, Scottish Arts Council [SAC] Award) and *Some Branch Against the Sky* (prose, David & Charles and Timber Press 1997).

He wrote much poetry on these explorations but published it rarely; his first collection pamphlet, *31 Poems* (Old Fire Station Poets, Oxford, 1977) was followed by three book-length collections, *Camp One* (Macdonald, 1978: SAC Award), *Squaring the Waves* (Bloodaxe Books, 1986: SAC Award) and *The Concrete Garden* (Bloodaxe Books, 1991: Poetry Book Society Recommendation), and what was was to be his swansong, *The Bare Abundance: Selected Poems 1975-2001* (Bloodaxe Books, 2002: Poetry Book Society Recommendation).